The E  Lover's Cookbook

Cooking, Grilling Baking with Brie: 40 Best Brie Recipes

BY

Christina Tosch

Copyright 2019 Christina Tosch

Copyright Notes

This Book may not be reproduced, in part or in whole, without explicit permission and agreement by the Author by any means. This includes but is not limited to print, electronic media, scanning, photocopying or file sharing.

The Author has made every effort to ensure accuracy of information in the Book but assumes no responsibility should personal or commercial damage arise in the case of misinterpretation or misunderstanding. All suggestions, instructions and guidelines expressed in the Book are meant for informational purposes only, and the Reader assumes any and all risk when following said information.

vvvvvvvvvvvvvvvvvvvvvvvvvvvvvvvvvvvvvvvvvvv

A special thank you for purchasing my book!

My sincerest thanks for purchasing my book! As added thanks, you are now eligible to receive a complimentary book sent to your email every week. To get started on this exclusive offer, fill in the box below by entering your email address and start receiving notifications of special promotions. It's not every day you get something for free for doing so little! Free and discounted books are available every day and a reminder will be sent to you so you never have to miss out. Fill in the box below and get started on this amazing offer!

https://christina.subscribemenow.com

Table of Contents

Introduction 8

First Course 10

    Bacon, Brie and Basil Pasta 11

    Bacon-Wrapped Scallops with Brie and Creamy Sage Sauce 14

    Baked Brie with Figs, Pistachios, and Orange 17

    Brie Toast with Roasted Grapes 20

    Cherry-Brandy Baked and Boozy Brie 22

    Cranberry Brie and Orange Pie 24

    Honey Brie Brûlée 27

    Olive and Brie Tapenade Nachos 29

    Shrimp and Baked Brie 32

    Spinach and Brie Dip 35

Main Course 39

Apricot Glazed Walnut and Brie Stuffed Chicken with Roast Potatoes 40

Baked Salmon with Brie and Mango 44

Brie and Bacon Risotto 47

Brie, Breadcrumb, and Parsley Topped Lamb Chops with Sweet Potato Mash 50

Brie-Filled Sausages with Onion and Herb Marmalade 53

Cheese Stuffed Pork Chops with Caramelized Green Apples and Toasted Walnuts 56

Cranberry Brie Turkey Pizza 59

Crunchy Breadcrumb-Topped Whiting with Brie 61

Ham and Brie Puff Pastry Parcel 64

Steak with Brie and Mushrooms 67

Soups, Salads, and Sides 70

Brie-Stuffed Artichokes 71

Cherry Tomatoes in Brie Sauce 74

Creamy Garlic and Brie Mushrooms 76

Herby Brie and Roast Garlic Soup 78

Honey-Dijon Chicken Salad with Pear, Brie, and Walnuts.. 81

Louisiana Crab and Brie Soup 84

Spiced Fruity Chutney Topped Brie with Toasted Pecans 88

Tomato and Brie Focaccia.. 91

Warm Duck Salad with Brie Toast 95

White Truffle and Brie Stuffed Crispy Potatoes 98

Dessert.. 101

Apple, Fig, and Brie Skillet Tart 102

Baked Peaches and Brie with Honey Drizzle.............. 105

Blueberry, Brie, and Walnut Scones 107

Brie Ice Cream with Roast Strawberries 110

Bruleed Banana, Brie and Gingersnap Stacks............ 113

Fig and Brie S'mores 116

Nutty Crepes with Burnt Honey and Brie 118

Salted Chocolate Covered Brie Bites 121

White Chocolate and Orange Brie Cups 123

Yogurt and Brie Panna Cotta with Passion Fruit Sauce 125

Author's Afterthoughts 128

About the Author 129

Introduction

Brie is one of the world's greatest and most popular cheeses and that's not just down to its taste.

Not only is it perfect on a plate to enjoy with crackers but it's also delicious baked in the oven, perfect wrapped in pastry, and a versatile ingredient for soups, salads, and even desserts.

Whether you are cooking, grilling or baking, Brie is the perfect partner in lots of different recipes from appetizers to soups to salads, sides, mains, and desserts.

But before you say yes please to cheese, here are some un-Brie-lievabley fascinating facts:

- One of the best known French cheeses, Brie is often called the Queen of Cheeses
- A soft cheese, Brie comes from the French region of the same name
- In the majority of countries, Brie-style cheeses are produced using pasteurized milk
- History tells that French king, Louis XVI's final dying wish was to have one final taste of, you guessed it, Brie cheese

The Brie Cheese-Lover's Cookbook brings together a collection of the 40 Best Brie Recipes to get you cooking, grilling and baking with Brie!

First Course

Bacon, Brie and Basil Pasta

Add this delicious pasta recipe to your weekday meal plan – it's easy to prepare and takes just half an hour from pan to plate.

Servings: 4

Total Time: 30mins

Ingredients

- 10 ounces pasta
- 4 pieces thickly- sliced bacon
- ½ yellow onion (peeled, thinly sliced)
- 2 cloves garlic (peeled, minced)
- 1 (8 ounce) wheel Brie (cut into cubes)
- 10-12 basil leaves (cut into a chiffonade)
- Sea salt and freshly cracked black pepper

Directions:

1. Cook the pasta in salted boiling water until al dente. Set ½ a cup of the pasta cooking water to one side. Drain the pasta and set aside.

2. Over moderate heat, add the bacon to a skillet and cook on both sides until crisp and brown.

3. Remove the bacon from the skillet and put aside to cool on a plate lined with kitchen paper.

4. Once the bacon is cooled, break it into bite-size pieces.

5. Add the onion to the bacon fat and over moderate-high heat, sauté for 5 minutes, until caramelized.

6. Add the garlic and toss for 30-40 seconds, until fragrant.

7. Add the cubes of cheese along with a ½ cup of the pasta cooking water set aside earlier and continuously stir until the cheese is entirely melted.

8. Add the drained pasta to the pan and toss to combine.

9. Add the basil and season to taste.

10. Enjoy.

Bacon-Wrapped Scallops with Brie and Creamy Sage Sauce

subtle sage and cream sauce is the perfect choice for delicately-flavored scallops and salty bacon.

Servings: 2

Total Time: 40mins

Ingredients:

- 1 pint half and half
- 6 rashers of smoked bacon
- 6 sea scallops (cleaned)
- 1 tsp salt (divided)
- 1 tsp black pepper (divided)
- 1 tbsp extra-virgin olive oil
- 4 ounces Brie cheese (cut into small pieces)
- 2-4 sage leaves (coarsely chopped)
- ¼ tsp ground nutmeg

Directions:

1. Preheat the main oven to 350 degrees F.

2. In a pan of 2-quart capacity, over moderate heat, heat the half and half, until reduced by 50 percent. Take care that it doesn't boil over and skim and discard any surface foam, regularly.

3. In the meantime, arrange the bacon on a cookie sheet and bake in the oven for 3-5 minutes.

4. Pat the cleaned scallops dry with kitchen paper towel and season with ½ tsp each of salt and pepper.

5. Take the bacon out of the oven and allow to cool.

6. In a frying pan, heat the oil until hot.

7. In the meantime, wrap the scallops in one piece of the cooled bacon, securing them with cocktail sticks.

8. Add the scallops to the pan and cook on each side for 2 minutes.

9. Remove the scallops from the pan and return to the baking sheet. Place the baking sheets in the oven for between 3-5 minutes, or until just cooked through.

10. While the scallops are in the oven, add the Brie along with the sage to the half and half and whisk until entirely melted and combined.

11. Season the sauce with the remaining ½ teaspoons of salt and pepper along with the nutmeg. It may be necessary at this stage to strain the sauce through a mesh sieve.

12. Drizzle the sauce over the scallops, garnish with sage and enjoy.

Baked Brie with Figs, Pistachios, and Orange

Get a group of friends together and tuck into this baked Brie.

Servings: 8-10

Total Time: 30mins

Ingredients:

- 1 (8 ounce) wheel of Brie
- ¼ cup fig preserves
- ¼ cup figs (sliced)
- ½ cup pistachios (chopped)
- Zest of 1 medium-size orange
- Freshly ground black pepper (to season)
- 1 tbsp runny honey
- 1 tbsp fresh thyme (chopped)
- Crackers (to serve)

Directions:

1. Preheat the main oven to 375 degrees F.

2. Add the Brie to an oven-proof skillet and place the skillet on a cookie sheet.

3. In a bowl, combine the preserves with the figs, pistachios and orange zest, stirring to incorporate fully.

4. Spoon the mixture over the surface of the cheese.

5. Season with black pepper and place the skillet in the preheated oven.

6. Bake the Brie for 15-18 minutes, until heated through.

7. Remove the Brie from the oven and drizzle with runny honey.

8. Serve, garnished with fresh thyme and alongside a bowl of crackers.

Brie Toast with Roasted Grapes

This delicious finger food or appetizers pair perfectly with wine, beer, or soda.

Servings: 4-6

Total Time: 25mins

Ingredients:

- 1 pound seedless grapes
- 1 tbsp extra-virgin olive oil
- Salt and freshly ground black pepper
- 6-8 ounces Brie cheese (cut into 16 slices)
- 12 (¼" thick) slices of crusty French loaf (toasted)

Directions:

1. Preheat the main oven to 375 degrees F.

2. Line a baking sheet with parchment paper.

3. In a single layer, arrange the grapes on the prepared baking sheet. Drizzle with oil and season.

4. Place in the preheated oven and roast for 18-20 minutes, until soft and wrinkled. Set aside to cool.

5. Place 1 slice of Brie on top of each slice of toasted French loaf. Top each slice of toast with a small handful of roasted grapes, drizzling over any grape juice that has collected on the baking sheet.

6. Serve and enjoy.

Cherry-Brandy Baked and Boozy Brie

Cherry brandy adds depth of flavor to salty French Brie baked in the oven.

Servings: 6-8

Total Time: 20mins

Ingredients:

- 1 (8 ounce) wheel of French Brie
- ½ cup dried cherries
- ½ cup chopped walnuts
- ¼ cup packed brown sugar
- ¼ cup cherry brandy
- French bread baguette (toasted, to serve)

Directions:

1. Preheat the main oven to 350 degrees F

2. Place the Brie cheese on a 9" pie plate. In a bowl, combine the cherries with the walnuts, brown sugar and brandy and spoon the mixture evenly over cheese.

3. Bake in the oven at 15-20 minutes, until cheese is softened.

4. Serve with warm, crusty baguette.

Cranberry Brie and Orange Pie

Bright red cranberries and freshly squeezed orange juice provide a tart tang to a mellow Brie cheese pie.

Servings: 12

Total Time: 1hour 35mins

Ingredients:

- 3 cups fresh or frozen cranberries
- 1 cup packed brown sugar
- 1 cup freshly squeezed orange juice
- ⅓ cup all-purpose flour
- 1 tsp balsamic vinegar
- 1 sheet of refrigerated pie crust
- 4 ounces Brie cheese (finely chopped)
- 1 tsp vanilla essence
- 2 tbsp butter

Topping:

- ½ cup all-purpose flour
- ¼ cup packed brown sugar
- ¼ cup cold butter (cut into cubes)

Directions:

1. Preheat the main oven to 450 degrees F.

2. In a pan, combine the cranberries with the brown sugar, freshly squeezed orange juice, flour, and balsamic vinegar.

3. Over moderate heat, cook until the berries begin to pop, for approximately 15 minutes.

4. In the meantime, unroll the crust into a 9" pie plate.

5. Sprinkle with cheese and bake in the oven for 6-8 minutes until the Brie begins to melt.

6. Turn the temperature of the oven down to 350 degrees F.

7. Take the cranberry mixture off the heat and stir in the vanilla essence.

8. Pour the mixture into the crust and dot with butter.

9. To prepare the topping: In a bowl, combine the flour with the brown sugar and cut into the butter until crumbly. Sprinkle the mixture evenly over the filling.

10. Bake in the oven for 30-35 minutes, until the crust is golden and the filling bubbles. You may need to cover the edges of the crust with aluminum foil during the final 20 minutes of baking to prevent over-browning.

11. Serve the pie warm and enjoy.

Honey Brie Brûlée

This savory Brie benefits from the flavor and texture of sweet and sticky honey to share with friends.

Servings: 4-6

Total Time: 12mins

Ingredients:

- 1 (8 ounce) wheel of triple Brie (top and rind removed)
- 1 tbsp honey
- 1 tbsp turbinado sugar
- Honey (to drizzle)
- Crostini (to serve)

Directions:

1. Preheat the broiler

2. Place the Brie on a heat-safe plate, cut side facing upwards.

3. Spread the honey evenly over the surface of the Brie and top with an even layer of turbinado sugar.

4. Place the Brie under the grill and grill for approximately 60 seconds, until the sugar entirely melts and caramelizes.

5. Remove the Brie from the heat and allow the sugar to harden and cool, for 1-2 minutes.

6. Drizzle with honey and serve with crostini.

Olive and Brie Tapenade Nachos

Serve these tasty nachos as an appetizer or savory snack.

Servings: 2

Total Time: 35mins

Ingredients:

- ½ cup canola oil
- 6 corn tortillas (cut into 6 triangles)
- ½ tsp chipotle chili powder
- 4 pinches of salt
- 5 ounces Brie cheese (rind removed, cut into cubes)
- ½ cup store-bought olive tapenade
- 1 green onion (chopped)
- 1 tbsp cilantro (chopped)

Directions:

1. Preheat the main oven to 350 degrees F.

2. Over moderate heat, heat a skillet and add the oil.

3. Place a corner of one of the tortilla chips in the oil, and if it begins to bubble the oil is sufficiently hot.

4. In batches, add the remaining tortilla chips.

5. Using kitchen tongs, flip the chips over as soon as their undersides turn a pale golden color.

6. As soon as the chips are golden all over, remove them from the pan and transfer to a kitchen paper towel-lined platter.

7. Sprinkle the chili powder and salt evenly over the chips and place them in an oven-safe dish. The chips need to be placed, so they stand up as this makes them easier to coat with melted cheese.

8. Scatter the cheese all over the chips and bake in the oven until it entirely melts.

9. Remove from the oven and top with the store-bought olive tapenade.

10. Garnish with onion and chopped cilantro.

11. Serve and enjoy.

Shrimp and Baked Brie

Cheese often overwhelms the flavor of delicate seafood, but this is not the case in this recipe where mild Brie compliments juicy shrimp perfectly.

Servings: 3-4

Total Time: 22mins

Ingredients:

- ¼ cup butter (softened)
- 3 tbsp olive oil
- 2 tbsp freshly squeezed lemon juice
- 2 cloves garlic (peeled, minced)
- 1 tsp black pepper
- 2 tbsp dried oregano
- 1 tsp sea salt
- 1 small wheel of Brie
- 6-12 medium-size shrimp (peeled, deveined)
- ¼ cup parsley (chopped)
- Almonds (to serve, optional)
- Scallions (to serve, optional)
- Tomatoes (diced, to serve, optional)
- Crusty bread (to serve, optional)

Directions:

1. Preheat the main oven to 350 degrees F.

2. In a bowl, combine the softened butter with the oil, fresh lemon juice, garlic, black pepper, oregano, and salt. Set to one side.

3. Place the cheese in an oven-proof baking dish along with the shrimp and ⅓ of the butter mixture and bake in the preheated oven until the Brie is softened, for approximately 12-15 minutes.

4. Top with parsley, almonds, scallion, and tomatoes and serve with crusty bread.

Spinach and Brie Dip

A rich and creamy cheese dip is a great addition to any get-together or party.

Servings: 15

Total Time: 30mins

Ingredients:

- 4 tbsp unsalted butter
- ¼ onion (peeled, chopped)
- 2-3 garlic cloves (peeled, minced)
- ¼ cup all-purpose flour
- 2 cups milk
- 1 tsp Worcestershire sauce
- ½ tsp salt
- ½ tsp pepper
- ¼ tsp paprika
- ¼ tsp cayenne
- ½ cup sour cream
- 1 (10 ounce) package frozen spinach (thawed, squeezed dry)
- 1 cup chopped roasted red peppers (thoroughly drained, patted dry)
- 1 (13 ounce) wheel of Brie cheese (rind removed, cut into cubes)
- 1 cup mozzarella cheese (freshly grated, divided)
- ¾ cup Pepper Jack cheese (freshly grated, divided)
- ½ cup Parmesan cheese (freshly grated, divided)

Directions:

1. Preheat the main oven to 375 degrees F.

2. Over moderate-high heat, melt the butter in a 9" oven-safe frying pan.

3. Add the onions and while stirring, cook for a few minutes.

4. Add the garlic and sauté for 30 seconds.

5. Stir in the flour and while stirring, cook for 2 minutes.

6. Reduce the heat down to low and stir in the milk along with the Worcestershire sauce, salt, pepper, paprika, and cayenne. Turn the heat up to moderately high and while stirring, bring to simmer until slightly thickened.

7. Remove from the heat and stir in the sour cream until silky smooth.

8. Stir in the spinach along with the roasted peppers, Brie, a ½ cup of mozzarella, ½ cups of Pepper Jack cheese, and a ¼ cup of Parmesan cheese.

9. Smooth the dip into an even layer and top with the remaining Brie, mozzarella, Pepper Jack and Parmesan cheese and broil until golden.

10. Allow to sit for 5 minutes before serving with crusty bread.

Main Course

Apricot Glazed Walnut and Brie Stuffed Chicken with Roast Potatoes

This restaurant-worthy main will impress your family and friends.

Servings: 4

Total Time: 1hour 5mins

Ingredients:

Potatoes:

- 1½ pounds small-size purple and red potatoes (cut in half)
- 3-4 tbsp olive oil
- 1 tsp seasoned salt
- ½ tsp black pepper
- 2 cloves garlic (peeled, grated)
- Zest of 1 fresh lemon

Chicken:

- ½ cup walnuts (lightly toasted)
- 1 cup fresh basil
- 1 clove garlic (peeled, minced)
- 2 tbsp olive oil (divided)
- 6 ounces Brie cheese (cut into cubes)
- 2 ounces cream cheese
- 1 egg
- ½ tsp salt
- ½ tsp black pepper
- ¼ tsp crushed red pepper
- 4 skin-on boneless chicken breast

- ¾ cup apricot preserves
- 1 tbsp balsamic vinegar

Directions:

1. Preheat the main oven to 400 degrees F.

2. Arrange the potatoes on a large baking tray, drizzle with oil and season with salt, pepper, garlic, and lemon zest. Toss to coat evenly.

3. Roast the potatoes in the oven for 10 minutes.

4. In the meantime, prepare the chicken: Add the walnuts, basil, and garlic to a food blender and gradually add the tablespoon of oil, until the mixture has a paste-like consistency.

5. Add the Brie, along with the cream cheese and egg to the processor and on pulse, mix to combine. Season with salt, black pepper, and red pepper.

6. Carefully pull the skin up and away from the chicken.

7. Spread between 1-2 tbsp of the Brie mixture under the skin of each chicken breast.

8. Take the potatoes out of the oven and push the potatoes to one side on the baking tray.

9. Place the chicken on the tray alongside the potatoes.

10. Add the apricot preserves and the balsamic vinegar, and 1 tbsp of oil to a bowl and stir to combine. Spread this mixture over the surface of the breasts.

11. Return the baking tray to the oven and roast for between 30-40 minutes until the chicken is sufficiently cooked through and the potatoes are fork-tender. You may need to remove the potatoes from the oven earlier than the chicken.

12. Serve and enjoy.

Baked Salmon with Brie and Mango

The perfect recipe for fish-lovers, baked salmon topped with Brie and topped with cooked, softened mangos.

Servings: 4

Total Time: 50mins

Ingredients:

- 2 tbsp olive oil
- 4 (4 ounce) salmon fillets
- 4 ounces Brie cheese (sliced)
- 1 tsp butter
- 2 ripe mangos (peeled, seeded, diced)

Directions:

1. Preheat the main oven to 350 degrees F.

2. Over moderate-high heat, in an oven-safe skillet, heat the oil.

3. Add the salmon to the skillet and sear on both sides; this will take 6-8 minutes in total.

4. Top the salmon fillets with the Brie and cover the skillet with a lid before transferring it to the oven.

5. Bake in the oven for 15 minutes or until the fish flakes easily when using a fork.

6. In a pan, over moderate heat, melt the butter.

7. Add the mangos to the pan and simmer until softened, for 15 minutes.

8. Serve the mangos on top of the salmon and enjoy.

Brie and Bacon Risotto

Slowly does it when cooking risotto, but your patience will be well rewarded once you taste this delicious risotto.

Servings: 2

Total Time: 40mins

Ingredients:

- 5 ounces bacon (chopped into small cubes)
- 1 chicken stock cube
- 2 cups water (boiling)
- 1 Spanish red onion (peeled, finely chopped)
- 6 ounces rice
- 2-3 ounces Brie cheese (chopped)
- Apple sauce (store-bought, to serve, optional)
- Handful of fresh parsley (chopped)

Directions:

1. Using a colander, rinse the cubes of bacon under cold water and using kitchen paper towel, pat dry.

2. Dissolve the chicken stock cube in the boiling water.

3. Add the bacon to a dry frying pan along with the onion and bring to low heat. Cook until the onion is softened and bacon has released its fat.

4. Once the fat is nearly translucent, add the rice, while stirring to coat the edges. Cook until the ends of the rice grains are beginning to become clear and pour in the stock one ladleful at a time, stirring to combine.

5. Allow the rice to absorb the liquid as it cooks and continue to gradually and add the remaining chicken stock, as it absorbs the rice. You may not need to use all of the chicken stock as you aiming for a soup-like, al dente consistency. This will take around 20 minutes.

6. When you are ready to serve fold in the Brie until it mostly melts.

7. Swirl in a little apple sauce, garnish with chopped parsley and serve.

Brie, Breadcrumb, and Parsley Topped Lamb Chops with Sweet Potato Mash

Chargrilled, juicy lamb chops topped with ooey gooey cheese and crunchy breadcrumbs is the perfect weekend meal to share.

Servings: 2

Total Time: 35mins

Ingredients:

Lamb Chops:

- Dash of olive oil
- 2 lamb chops
- Sea salt and black pepper

Topping:

- 2 ounces Brie cheese (chopped)
- 2 tbsp fresh white breadcrumbs
- 1 tbsp fresh parsley (chopped)
- 1 tbsp fresh mint (chopped)
- Salt and black pepper

Sweet Potato Mash:

- 1 sweet potato (peeled, chopped)
- 1 ounce butter
- 1 tbsp milk
- Salt and black pepper

Directions:

1. Preheat the main oven to 400 degrees F.

2. In an oven-safe frying pan, heat the oil.

3. Season the lamb chops with sea salt and black pepper and fry each side for 2-3 minutes, until golden.

4. To prepare the topping: In a bowl, combine the Brie with the breadcrumbs, parsley, and mint. Season with salt and pepper and evenly spread the mixture on top of the chops.

5. Bake in the oven for 5 minutes, until the lamb is cooked to your preferred doneness and the topping is golden.

6. For the mash: Cook the potato in boiling water for between 6-8 minutes, until fork-tender.

7. Drain the potatoes and mash with butter and milk until silky smooth. Season to taste and serve alongside the lamb chops.

Brie-Filled Sausages with Onion and Herb Marmalade

Sausages get a makeover with a melted brie filling and homemade onion and herb marmalade.

Servings: 2-3

Total Time: 45mins

Ingredients:

Marmalade:

- 1¾ tbsp unsalted butter
- 2 red onions (peeled, thinly sliced)
- 3 celery stalks (trimmed, thinly sliced)
- 1 tsp fresh thyme leaves
- 1 tbsp brown sugar
- 1 cup dry red wine
- ¼ cup red wine vinegar
- ¼ cup redcurrant jelly

Sausages:

- 6 premium, thick pork sausages
- 4½ ounces Brie (cut into ¼" slices)
- Mixed green salad leaves (to serve, optional)

Directions:

1. Over moderate heat, melt the butter in a pan.

2. Add the onion along with the celery and cook while stirring, until softened, for 5-6 minutes.

3. Next, add the thyme leaves and brown sugar and while stirring, caramelize; for approximately 5 minutes.

4. Pour in the red wine and vinegar and cook for an additional 10-15 minutes while occasionally stirring, until thickened.

5. Add the jelly and stir well until entirely melted. Set to one side.

6. Preheat your grill to high heat.

7. Add the sausages to the grill and cook, while turning for 6-8 minutes, until sufficiently cooked all over.

8. Split each sausage lengthways, making sure not to cut all the way through.

9. Fill the sausage with the Brie cheese and return to the grill for a couple of minutes, until the cheese is just melted.

10. Serve with the onions marmalade and mixed salad leaves.

Cheese Stuffed Pork Chops with Caramelized Green Apples and Toasted Walnuts

Sweet and spicy these pork chops are delicious. So, what are you waiting for? Get baking with Brie.

Servings: 2

Total Time: 35mins

Ingredients:

- 2 bone-in pork chops (butterflied)
- 1 (8 ounce) wheel of Brie (cut into slices)
- Olive oil
- ½ onion (peeled, diced)
- 2 Granny Smith apples
- 2 tbsp sugar
- 1 tbsp runny honey
- 1 tsp rice wine vinegar
- 1 tsp sambal spice paste
- ¼ cup walnuts (chopped)

Directions:

1. Preheat the main oven to 425 degrees F.

2. Stuff the butterflied pork chops with slices of Brie cheese.

3. In a frying pan, sear the chops for 4 minutes on each side.

4. Transfer the chops to the preheated oven for 3 minutes.

5. In a second pan, heat the oil.

6. Add the onions along with the apples to the pan and on moderate heat, cook for 8-12 minutes, until softened.

7. Next, add the sugar and honey to the pan and cook until caramelized and entirely incorporated.

8. Stir in the vinegar and sambal paste and cook for an additional couple of minutes.

9. Fold in the chopped nuts and spoon the mixture over the pork chops.

10. Enjoy.

Cranberry Brie Turkey Pizza

Now you can enjoy all the flavors of a Thanksgiving dinner but with the convenience of a store-bought pizza base.

Servings: 2-4

Total Time: 20mins

Ingredients:

- 1 cup cranberry sauce
- 1 (12") thin and crispy pizza crust
- 1 (8 ounce) wheel of Brie
- 1 cup leftover, cooked turkey (cut into large cubes)
- ½ cup pecans (chopped)

Directions:

1. Preheat the main oven to 425 degrees F.

2. Evenly spread the cranberry sauce over the pizza base.

3. Pull off small pieces from half of the Brie cheese wheel and arrange them over the sauce.

4. Scatter the cubes of cooked turkey over the Brie. Top with the remaining Brie and garnish with pecans.

5. Bake in the preheated oven for 10 minutes, until the Brie melts and the sauce bubbles.

6. Set aside to stand for a few minutes before serving.

Crunchy Breadcrumb-Topped Whiting with Brie

Filled with Brie and with a crunchy breadcrumb topping this fish main course is packed full of flavor. Serve with a crisp green salad and enjoy.

Servings: 2-4

Total Time: 40mins

Ingredients:

- 4 (5-6 ounce) whiting fillets
- 1 ounce butter (melted)
- Salt and black pepper (to season)
- 2 ounces Brie cheese (softened, sliced)
- 2 ounces fresh breadcrumbs
- 3 tbsp parsley (chopped)
- Zest of 1 fresh lemon
- 1-2 tbsp olive oil

Directions:

1. Preheat the main oven to 400 degrees F.

2. Arrange the fish, skin side facing upwards on a cutting board and brush with melted butter — season with salt and pepper.

3. Place ½ ounce of Brie on top of each fillet.

4. Roll the fillet up and place on a lightly greased, oven-safe dish. Brush with any remaining melted butter.

5. To prepare the topping: In a bowl, combine the breadcrumbs with the parsley, lemon zest, and oil. Spoon the mixture evenly over the fish.

6. Bake in the oven for between 20-25 minutes, until the fish flakes easily when using a fork.

7. Serve and enjoy.

Ham and Brie Puff Pastry Parcel

Puffy pastry encases deli ham and gooey Brie to deliver a tasty midweek main or weekend supper.

Servings: 8

Total Time: 50mins

Ingredients:

- 1 (8ounce) wheel of Brie
- 4 slices delicatessen ham
- All-purpose flour (to roll)
- 1 sheet of puff pastry (defrosted)
- 1 large-size egg, whisked with ½ tsp milk

Directions:

1. Preheat the main oven to 400 degrees F.

2. Arrange the wheel of Brie on a chopping board. Lay the ham slices on top of the cheese, slightly overlapping one another. Tuck the ham underneath the wheel and put to one side.

3. Lightly dust a clean work surface with flour.

4. Roll the puff pastry out onto the work surface. It needs to be large enough to provide a 3½" border around the cheese when placed in the middle.

5. Place the Brie in the middle of the pastry and carefully fold the pastry up and around the cheese with the seam on the bottom. Trim off any excess underneath as necessary.

6. Re-roll the excess pastry and with a ruler and pizza cutter. Cut thin strips of pastry. Lay the strips diagonally across the pastry covered wheel of Brie to form a diamond pattern.

7. Brush the egg wash all over the pastry,

8. Lay the Brie on a baking sheet, lined with parchment paper and place I the preheated oven for 20-25 minutes, until golden.

9. Set aside for several minutes before serving.

Steak with Brie and Mushrooms

If you are planning a special occasion, then this dish is sure to impress – a restaurant-worthy main without breaking the bank.

Servings: 4

Total Time: 20mins

Ingredients:

- 4 (1"thick) filet mignon steaks
- 1 tbsp vegetable oil
- Salt and black pepper
- 3½ ounces Brie cheese (cut into 4 slices)
- 1 tbsp olive oil
- 3½ ounces Beech mushrooms
- ¼ cup dry white wine

Directions:

1. Rub the steaks all over with oil and season on both sides with salt and black pepper.

2. Place a large skillet over moderate-high heat, and heat until very hot.

3. Add the steaks to the hot pan and gently but firmly press them into the pan to ensure their whole surface comes into contact with the hot pan. Leave the pan undisturbed until the steaks are cooked one-third of the way up the sides.

4. Turn the steaks over and lay a slice of cheese on top of each one.

5. Continue to cook the steak until it is cooked to your preferred level of doneness.

6. Remove the steaks from the pan and set to one side.

7. Add 1 tbsp of oil to the pan together with the mushrooms and cook until the mushrooms are beginning to brown and wilt.

8. Pour in the wine and allow the mixture to boil until virtually evaporated — season with salt and pepper.

9. Top each steak with the mushrooms and enjoy.

Soups, Salads, and Sides

Brie-Stuffed Artichokes

Yummy artichokes stuffed with Brie cheese and topped with crisp golden breadcrumbs are the ultimate accompaniment to your favorite meat, poultry, and fish dishes.

Servings: 3

Total Time: 40mins

Ingredients:

- 3 large artichokes
- Nonstick cooking spray
- 8 ounces Brie (rind removed, cut into chunks)
- ⅓ cup heavy whipping cream
- Yolk of 1 medium egg
- ½ cup Parmesan cheese (grated)
- Black pepper
- ⅓ cup plain breadcrumbs
- 2 tbsp salted butter
- 1 tbsp dried thyme

Directions:

1. Bring a large pot of salty water to a boil.

2. Cut and discard the top third of the artichokes and place the remaining artichoke pieces in the water. Boil for 10 minutes then drain away the water.

3. Spritz a 9" pie dish with nonstick spray and arrange the artichokes upright inside.

4. In a saucepan over low heat, warm the Brie until creamy and smooth. Turn off the heat and add in the cream, egg yolk and half of the Parmesan cheese while continually stirring. Season to taste with black pepper.

5. Preheat your oven's broiler to low heat and arrange a rack in the bottom of the oven.

6. Fill each artichoke with the Brie mixture.

7. In a clean bowl combine the breadcrumbs, salted butter, and dried thyme with the remaining Parmesan cheese and scatter the mixture over the top of the filled artichokes.

8. Place under the broiler for approximately 4 minutes until crisp and golden.

Cherry Tomatoes in Brie Sauce

This tasty tomato and Brie side dish will add color and flavor to lots of different meat and poultry dishes.

Servings: 6-8

Total Time: 15mins

Ingredients:

- 16 ounces Brie cheese
- 1 cup milk
- 1 cup light cream
- Pinch of fresh basil
- Pinch of rosemary
- Pinch of thyme
- 36 ounces cherry tomatoes

Directions:

1. In a pan, combine the Brie with the milk and cream, and over very low heat, and while constantly stirring melt the cheese.

2. Season with the herbs (basil, rosemary, and thyme).

3. Arrange the cherry tomatoes on a platter and top with the Brie sauce.

4. Serve and enjoy.

Creamy Garlic and Brie Mushrooms

This simple yet delicious dish pairs perfectly with a well cooked steak.

Servings: 4

Total Time: 20mins

Ingredients:

- 1 tbsp butter
- 1 pound mushrooms
- 2 garlic cloves (peeled, chopped)
- ¼ cup vegetable broth
- 4 ounces Brie cheese (rind removed)
- Salt and black pepper

Directions:

1. Over moderate heat, in a pan, heat the butter.

2. Add the mushrooms and cook until fork-tender, for 10-15 minutes.

3. Add the garlic and cook until fragrant, for 60 seconds.

4. Pour in the broth and add the Brie, cooking until the cheese melts.

5. Season with salt and pepper and serve.

Herby Brie and Roast Garlic Soup

This delicious soup packs a powerful flavor punch, serve with warm crusty bread for a yummy appetizer or lunch.

Servings: 6

Total Time: 40mins

Ingredients:

- 2 garlic heads (unpeeled, separated into cloves)
- 6 tbsp olive oil
- 1 yellow onion (peeled, diced)
- 2 celery sticks (diced)
- 1 carrot (diced)
- ¼ cup all-purpose flour
- 6 cups chicken broth
- 1 tsp fresh oregano (chopped)
- ½ tsp fresh thyme (chopped)
- 7 ounces Brie (rind removed, chopped into pieces)
- Salt
- Ground white pepper

Directions:

1. Preheat the main oven to 325 degrees F.

2. Add the garlic to a glass baking dish and drizzle over a third of the olive oil. Cover with aluminum foil and bake for half an hour until very tender. Allow the garlic to completely cool.

3. Add the remaining oil to a saucepan over moderate heat and sauté the onion in it for 10 minutes. Add the celery and carrot, sauté for another 10 minutes.

4. Sprinkle in the flour and stir until combined with the veggies. Sauté for a few minutes before stirring in the chicken broth a little at a time.

5. Bring the mixture to a boil, stirring continually. Turn the heat down to moderately low and simmer for 15 minutes until the soup has thickened, stirring occasionally.

6. Peel the cooked, cooled garlic and transfer to a food processor along with a cup of the soup. Blitz until smooth. Return the mixture to the saucepan along with the fresh oregano and thyme.

7. Bring the soup to a simmer and add the Brie a little at a time until all of the cheese has melted. Stir well and season to taste with salt and white pepper. Serve.

Honey-Dijon Chicken Salad with Pear, Brie, and Walnuts

Jazz-up a regular grilled chicken salad with Brie, fresh pear and walnuts.

Servings: 4

Total Time: 45mins

Ingredients:

- 4 boneless chicken breasts

Marinade:

- 3 tbsp Dijon mustard
- 3 tbsp freshly squeezed lemon juice
- Pinch of salt
- Dash of pepper
- Honey-Dijon Glaze:
- 1 tsp cornstarch
- 3-4 tbsp water
- 4 tbsp Dijon mustard
- ¼ cup honey
- 1 tbsp freshly grated ginger
- 2 tbsp rice wine vinegar
- Pinch of salt
- ½ cup chicken stock

Salad:

- Baby salad greens
- 1 pear (cored, sliced)
- Walnuts (toasted)
- Brie cheese (cubed)

Directions:

1. For the marinade: In a bowl, combine all the marinade Ingredients (mustard, lemon juice, salt, and pepper).

2. Rub the marinade over the chicken and transfer to the fridge for 30 minutes to marinate.

3. In the meantime, prepare the glaze.

4. Combine the cornstarch with the water to create a slurry.

5. In a pan, bring the mustard, honey, ginger, vinegar, salt, and stock to simmer for 10 minutes before thickening with the cornstarch slurry. Simmer for 60 seconds while constantly stirring.

6. Grill the chicken breasts until fully cooked, brushing it 5-6 times during the final 2-3 minutes of cooking time.

7. Slice the grilled chicken and serve it on a bed of baby salad greens, pear slices, and walnuts. Drizzle with the remaining glaze and garnish with cubes of Brie cheese.

Louisiana Crab and Brie Soup

When you want to impress, reach for this delicious Southern recipe for crab and Brie soup, with all the big, bold flavor that makes Louisiana cuisine famous.

Servings: 8-10

Total Time: 1hour 45mins

Ingredients:

- 2 pound fresh Louisiana blue crabs
- 2 ounces olive oil
- 1 medium-size yellow onion (peeled, diced)
- 1 medium-size carrot (diced)
- 3 ribs of celery (diced)
- 1 clove of garlic (peeled, minced)
- 2 bay leaves
- 2 ounces brandy
- 1 cup white wine
- 2 quarts water
- ½ cup unsalted butter
- ¾ cup flour
- 8 cups heavy whipping cream
- 1 (8 ounce) wheel of Brie (rind removed, cut into 1" cubes)
- 1 tsp salt
- 1 tsp white pepper
- 1 tsp cayenne pepper
- 1 pound jumbo Louisiana lump crabmeat (picked over)

Directions:

1. With a hammer, crack open the crab shells to expose the meat.

2. In a 1-gallon stockpot, heat the oil and add the cracked crabs. Sauté for 5 minutes before adding the onion, carrots, celery and bay leaves and continue to sauté for an additional 5 minutes.

3. Add the brandy along with the wine and water and over moderate heat, bring to simmer. Cook for 45 minutes.

4. With a skimmer, remove the veggies and crab from the stock.

5. In a small frying pan, melt the butter.

6. Blend in the flour until creamy smooth and over low heat, simmer for 60 seconds.

7. Add the mixture to the stock and with a wire whisk, whisk until the roux dissolves.

8. Add the cream and simmer for 10 minutes.

9. Add the Brie to the stock while constantly stirring until the cheese entirely melts.

10. Taste and season the soup with salt, white pepper, and cayenne.

11. Strain the soup through a fine-mesh strainer.

12. Add the lump crabmeat, stir and enjoy.

Spiced Fruity Chutney Topped Brie with Toasted Pecans

Fruit chutney and warm Brie are a tried and tested combination but garnishing with toasted pecans and preparing homemade chutney will make this dish even more irresistible.

Servings: 10

Total Time: 40mins

Ingredients:

- ½ cup water
- ¼ cup dried cranberries
- ½ cup granulated sugar
- 1¼ cups mandarin orange segments (seeded, chopped)
- 1 tbsp fresh lemon juice
- Pinch each ground ginger and cloves
- ¼ tsp ground cinnamon
- 8 ounce Brie
- ¼ cup toasted pecans (chopped)
- Crackers (to serve)

Directions:

1. Preheat the main oven to 400 degrees F.

2. Bring the water to a boil in a saucepan over moderately high heat. Stir in the cranberries and take off the heat. Allow to stand for several minutes.

3. Drain the cranberries and set aside 1 tbsp of the cooking liquid.

4. Return the drained cranberries and 1 tbsp cooking liquid to the saucepan. Stir in the sugar, mandarin segments, lemon juice, ginger, cloves, and cinnamon. Bring the mixture to a boil.

5. Turn down to a simmer and cook for 5-10 minutes until the liquid is almost completely evaporated.

6. Arrange the Brie in a 9" pie dish and bake in the oven for approximately 10 minutes until softened.

7. Spoon the prepared chutney on top of the warm Brie and garnish with toasted pecans.

8. Serve straight away with crackers.

Tomato and Brie Focaccia

A side of tasty focaccia goes well with all number of Italian mains.

Servings: 12

Total Time: 1hour 35mins

Ingredients:

- 2½ -3 cups all-purpose flour
- 2 (¼ ounce) ounce packages quick-rise yeast
- 1 tsp sugar
- 1 tsp salt
- 1 cup water
- ¼ cup + 1 tbsp olive oil (divided)
- 1 (14½ ounce) can diced tomatoes (drained)
- 2 cloves garlic (peeled, minced)
- 1 tsp Italian seasoning
- 6 ounces Brie cheese (cut into ½" cubes)
- Olive oil
- Crushed red pepper flakes

Directions:

1. In a bowl, combine 2 cups of flour along with the yeast, sugar, and salt.

2. In a pan, heat the water along with a ¼ cup of oil to a temperature of 120-130 degrees F.

3. Add to the dry Ingredients and beat until just moistened.

4. Stir in a sufficient amount of the remaining flour to form a soft dough.

5. Turn the dough out onto a floured work surface and knead until smooth and elastic, for between 6-8 minutes.

6. Place the dough in a lightly greased blow, turning over once to grease the top.

7. Cover the dough and allow to rise for 20 minutes.

8. Preheat the main oven to 375 degrees F.

9. Punch the dough down and gently press it into a 13x9" greased baking pan.

10. Cover the pan and set aside to rest for 10 minutes.

11. In a bowl, combine the diced tomatoes with the garlic, Italian seasoning, and the remaining oil.

12. Spread over the dough and top with the cheese.

13. Bake in the oven for between 25-30 minutes, until golden.

14. Place the pan on a wire baking rack and serve with a drizzle of olive oil and a sprinkle of red pepper flakes.

Warm Duck Salad with Brie Toast

Thanks to delicious pan-fried duck breast and cheesy Brie toast, this salad is no lite bite but rather a wholesome and filling meal for any time of the day.

Servings: 3

Total Time: 40mins

Ingredients:

- 1 pound duck breast halves
- Salt and black pepper
- 6 slices fruit and nut bread
- 6 ounces Brie (sliced)
- 3 tbsp olive oil
- 1½ tbsp sherry wine vinegar
- 6 cups mixed baby greens
- ½ cup toasted walnuts (chopped)

Directions:

1. Place a large skillet over moderately high heat. Season the duck with salt and black pepper.

2. Arrange the duck breast halves skin side down in the skillet. Cook for 6 minutes on each side, or until cooked to medium.

3. Take off the heat and allow to stand for 5 minutes.

4. Toast the sliced bread and top each with a slice of Brie.

5. Whisk together the oil and vinegar and season to taste.

6. Add the greens to a large serving bowl. Pour over the prepared dressing and toss to combine.

7. Arrange the Brie toasts around the edge of the bowl.

8. Thinly slice the prepared duck and arrange in the center of the salad. Scatter over the walnuts and serve straight away!

White Truffle and Brie Stuffed Crispy Potatoes

Golden crispy potatoes are topped with an irresistible blend of melting Brie, white truffle oil, garlic, and fresh herbs.

Servings: 8

Total Time: 1 hour

Ingredients:

- 1½ pounds mixed baby potatoes
- 1 tbsp extra-virgin olive oil
- Salt and black pepper
- 3 tbsp melted butter
- 2 tbsp fresh thyme (chopped)
- 2 garlic cloves (peeled and grated)
- 8 ounces Brie (cut into small wedges)
- 2 tsp white truffle oil
- 8 sage leaves (pan-fried)
- Pink peppercorns (crushed)

Directions:

1. Preheat the main oven to 400 degrees F.

2. Toss together the potatoes, oil, salt, and black pepper on a baking sheet until combined. Transfer to the oven and cook for 20 minutes until fork-tender.

3. Gently smash the potatoes.

4. Quickly combine the melted butter, thyme, and garlic. Drizzle the mixture over the smashed potatoes and return to the oven for another 20 or so minutes until crispy and golden.

5. For the final 5 minutes, add a slice of Brie to each potato and continue to cook until the cheese melts.

6. Transfer to a serving plate, drizzle with white truffle oil and garnish with sage leaves and pink peppercorns.

Dessert

Apple, Fig, and Brie Skillet Tart

A classic apple tart is brought to life with sweet and sticky dried figs and melt in the mouth Brie.

Servings: 8

Total Time: 50mins

Ingredients:

- 3 tbsp butter (at room temperature)
- ¾ cup granulated sugar
- 2 large apples (cored, peeled, quartered)
- 1 cup dried figs (halved)
- ½ pound Brie (rind removed, sliced)
- 1 sheet prepared pie crust (chilled)

Directions:

1. Preheat the main oven to 425 degrees F.

2. Spread the butter into the base of a 10" oven-safe skillet. Scatter over the granulated sugar.

3. Arrange the apples in the skillet, round side facing down. Sprinkle over the halved figs.

4. Place the skillet on moderate heat and cook until the apples soften a little and the sugar caramelizes. This should take just over 10 minutes.

5. Take off the heat and arrange the sliced Brie on top of the mixture.

6. Place the pie crust on top and tuck the edges under.

7. Transfer the skillet to the oven, placing on an upper rack. Bake for just over 15 minutes until the pastry is golden.

8. Allow the tart to cool in the skillet for several minutes before transferring to a plate and serving warm.

Baked Peaches and Brie with Honey Drizzle

Peaches are the perfect fruit to bake alongside Brie thanks to their juicy sweetness. A honey drizzle and fresh basil leaves take this simple pairing to the next level.

Servings: 8

Total Time: 30mins

Ingredients:

- Butter (to grease)
- 1 (8 ounce) Brie round
- 3 small peaches (stoned, chopped)
- 3 tbsp honey
- Small handful fresh basil (thinly sliced)
- Almond cookies (to serve)

Directions:

1. Preheat the main oven to 350 degrees F.

2. Grease a 9" square baking tin. Place the Brie in the tin and top with the chopped peaches. Place in the oven for 10 minutes.

3. Turn on the broiler.

4. Drizzle 2 tbsp of honey over the cheese and peaches and place under the broiler, 3-4" away from the heat source, for 5 minutes until golden.

5. Transfer to a serving plate, drizzle over the remaining honey and scatter with fresh basil. Serve almond cookies alongside for dipping.

Blueberry, Brie, and Walnut Scones

Slather with butter while still warm from the oven and serve alongside a delicious hot cup of coffee or tea for the ultimate afternoon indulgence.

Servings: 8

Total Time: 50mins

Ingredients:

- 2 tbsp granulated sugar
- 2 cups all-purpose flour
- ¼ tsp salt
- 2 tsp baking powder
- 5 tbsp unsalted butter (chilled, cubed)
- 1 egg (beaten lightly)
- ½ cup whole milk (chilled)
- 4 ounces Brie (cut into pieces)
- 4 ounces fresh blueberries
- ½ cup walnuts (coarsely chopped)
- Flour (for worktop)
- Milk (for brushing)
- Coarse sugar (for topping)

Directions:

1. Preheat the main oven to 425 degrees F and cover a baking sheet with parchment paper.

2. Combine the granulated sugar, flour, salt, and baking powder. Cut in the butter using two knives, until only pea-sized lumps remain.

3. Combine the beaten egg and the milk and add to the flour mixture and combine. The mixture should come together as a sticky dough.

4. Gently fold in the Brie, blueberries, and walnuts until evenly incorporated.

5. Lightly flour a clean worktop and tip the dough out onto it. Pat out the dough until it is 1" thick. Cut into rounds or triangles.

6. Transfer the scones to the prepared baking sheet. Brush each scone with milk and sprinkle with sugar.

7. Place in the oven and bake for 15-20 minutes until golden. Allow to cool for a 5 minutes before serving.

Brie Ice Cream with Roast Strawberries

Gourmet Brie ice cream with roasted strawberry topping is the perfect way to cool off this summer.

Servings: 8-10

Total Time: 5hours 40mins

Ingredients:

- 5 ounces Brie
- 2 cups heavy cream
- 1 pound fresh strawberries (hulled and quartered)
- ¼ cup granulated sugar
- 1 (14 ounce) can sweetened condensed milk
- Pinch salt
- 2 tsp fresh vanilla

Directions:

1. Place a 5x9" loaf pan in the freezer to chill.

2. Freeze the Brie for approximately 20 minutes then remove the rind. Chop into small pieces.

3. Place a saucepan over moderate heat and add the cream. Bring to a simmer then take off the heat and stir in the Brie until it melts. Set to one side allow to completely cool.

4. Strain the mixture through a sieve and discard any large pieces. Transfer the cheese/cream to the refrigerator to chill.

5. Preheat the main oven to 350 degrees F. Toss the strawberries in the granulated sugar and transfer to a baking sheet covered with parchment.

6. Place in the oven and roast for just under half an hour. Take out of the oven and allow to completely cool.

7. In a mixing bowl, whisk together the condensed milk, salt, and vanilla. Set to one side.

8. Whip the cooled cream using an electric stand mixer until it can hold stiff peaks. Fold the whipped cream into the milk mixture until incorporated.

9. Pour the mixture into the chilled loaf tin and cover with plastic wrap. Pop in the freezer for a couple of hours.

10. Stir in the cooled roast strawberries. Cover with plastic wrap and return to the freezer for another few hours until solid.

11. Enjoy.

Bruleed Banana, Brie and Gingersnap Stacks

Spicy gingersnap cookies, cinnamon-sugar bruleed bananas, and creamy Brie are stacked to create the perfect pop-in-the-mouth treat for your next get together.

Servings: 8

Total Time: 30mins

Ingredients:

- 1 (6 ounce) log Brie
- ¾ cup granulated sugar
- ½ tsp cinnamon
- Pinch salt
- 4 ripe bananas (peeled, sliced)
- 10 gingersnap cookies

Directions:

1. Set the Brie out at room temperature for half an hour. Cut into 10 slices.

2. Combine the sugar, cinnamon, and salt in a shallow dish.

3. Toss the sliced banana in the cinnamon sugar until evenly coated. Transfer the coated banana to a baking sheet in a single, even layer.

4. Pass a kitchen blow torch over the banana until the sugar melts and caramelizes.

5. Arrange the gingersnap cookies on a serving platter and top with a slice of banana, followed by a round of Brie, and another slice of banana.

6. Serve straight away.

Fig and Brie S'mores

S'mores aren't just for the kids! This grownup take on the classic campfire treat is simple and sophisticated.

Servings: 12

Total Time: 15mins

Ingredients:

- Nonstick cooking spray
- 12 ounces Brie (rind on, cut into 12 cubes)
- 24 graham crackers
- ¾ cup fig jam

Directions:

1. Arrange a rack in the top third of the oven and preheat the broiler to high for 5-10 minutes.

2. Spritz a cookie sheet with nonstick spray.

3. Place the Brie on the cookie sheet and place under the broiler for 5 minutes, flip the cheese cubes over and broil another 5 minutes.

4. Arrange 12 graham crackers on a serving plate, top each cracker with 1 tbsp of fig jam and a Brie cube, top with another graham cracker. Repeat with the remaining **Ingredients** and serve straight away.

Nutty Crepes with Burnt Honey and Brie

Made with chestnut flour and hazelnut milk, these homemade crepes have a deliciously nutty flavor which is perfectly complimented with soft Brie and burnt honey.

Servings: 10

Total Time: 35mins

Ingredients:

- ¼ cup sweet rice flour
- ¾ cup chestnut flour
- 3 medium eggs
- 1½ cups hazelnut milk
- 2 tbsp unsalted butter (melted and cooled)
- ¼ tsp fresh grated nutmeg
- ¼ tsp kosher salt
- Butter (for cooking)
- 8 ounces soft Brie (sliced thinly)
- 3-4 tbsp honey

Directions:

1. Add the flours, eggs, milk, melted butter, nutmeg, and salt to a blender and blitz until smooth and combined.

2. Place a nonstick skillet over moderate heat and brush with butter.

3. Pour a ¼ cup of the prepared batter into the hot pan and tilt and turn the pan to distribute the batter evenly. Cook for 1-2 minutes until the edges of the batter begins to curl. Flip the crepe and arrange a few slices of Brie along one third of the crepe. Cook for another 60 seconds.

4. Roll up the crepe and transfer to a side plate.

5. Repeat with the remaining crepe batter and Brie, brushing the pan with more butter in between cooking.

6. Drizzle the honey over the rolled crepes and spread out evenly using a spatula.

7. Pass a kitchen blow torch over the honey until a handful of spots appear.

8. Serve straight away.

Salted Chocolate Covered Brie Bites

Forget chocolate covered strawberries or even raisins! Think outside the box with these salted chocolates covered Brie bites. The perfect after-dinner treat to impress your guests.

Servings: 24

Total Time: 35mins

Ingredients:

- 8 ounces Brie
- 12 ounces chocolate melts
- Sea salt flakes

Directions:

1. Pop the Brie in the freezer for 20 minutes then cut into 24 equal bite-sized pieces.

2. Cover a cookie sheet with aluminum foil and set to one side.

3. Melt the chocolate melts using packet instructions.

4. Using two forks, dip each piece of Brie in the melted chocolate until evenly coated. Place on the cookie sheet.

5. While the chocolate is still wet, sprinkle a pinch of sea salt flakes on to each Brie bite.

6. Allow the chocolate to set in the refrigerator or at room temperature. Store in an airtight container in the refrigerator until ready to serve.

White Chocolate and Orange Brie Cups

White chocolate, sticky orange marmalade, and Brie cheese may not seem like an obvious combination, but just one bite and you'll be coming back for more!

Servings: 15

Total Time: 30mins

Ingredients:

- 1 (1.9 ounce) package frozen mini phyllo cups
- 1½ ounces baking white chocolate (chopped)
- 2 ounces Brie (chopped)
- ⅓ cup orange marmalade

Directions:

1. Preheat the main oven to 350 degrees F.

2. Fill each tart shell with a little white chocolate followed by a piece or two of Brie. Top with a small spoonful of orange marmalade.

3. Arrange the phyllo cups on a cookie sheet and bake in the oven for several minutes until golden.

4. Serve warm.

Yogurt and Brie Panna Cotta with Passion Fruit Sauce

This isn't just any panna cotta! This classic Italian dessert is elevated to the next level thanks to yogurt and Brie, which combine for an irresistibly smooth and velvety texture.

Servings: 8

Total Time: 3hours 15mins

Ingredients:

- 4 ounces Brie (rind removed)
- ⅓ cup plain yogurt
- ¾ cup 35% cream
- ⅓ cup granulated sugar
- 1 (¼ ounce) sachet unflavored gelatin
- 1 cup passion fruit juice
- ½ tsp cornstarch
- 1 tbsp water

Directions:

1. Using a double boiler, heat the Brie together with the yogurt, stirring until gently combined and smooth. This should take approximately 5 minutes.

2. In a saucepan, heat together the cream and granulated sugar. Bring to a boil, before pouring over the cheese mixture and stirring to combine.

3. Dissolve the gelatin in a little water then warm in a microwave for several seconds to aid dissolving.

4. Pour the gelatin into the cream/cheese mixture straight away and stir well.

5. Divide the mixture into 8 small ramekins and chill for 2-3 hours until set.

6. In the meantime, add the passion fruit juice to a pan over moderately high heat and bring to a boil.

7. Combine the cornstarch and 1 tbsp water, then pour into the passion fruit juice. Whisk to combine and take off the heat. Allow to cool completely.

8. Transfer the set panna cottas to serving plates and pour over the passion fruit sauce. Serve straight away.

Author's Afterthoughts

I would like to express my deepest thanks to you, the reader, for making this investment in one my books. I cherish the thought of bringing the love of cooking into your home.

With so much choice out there, I am grateful you decided to Purch this book and read it from beginning to end.

Please let me know by submitting an Amazon review if you enjoyed this book and found it contained valuable information to help you in your culinary endeavors. Please take a few minutes to express your opinion freely and honestly. This will help others make an informed decision on purchasing and provide me with valuable feedback.

Thank you for taking the time to review!

Christina Tosch

About the Author

Christina Tosch is a successful chef and renowned cookbook author from Long Grove, Illinois. She majored in Liberal Arts at Trinity International University and decided to pursue her passion of cooking when she applied to the world renowned Le Cordon Bleu culinary school in Paris, France. The school was lucky to recognize the immense talent of this chef and she excelled in her courses, particularly Haute Cuisine. This skill was recognized and rewarded by several highly regarded Chicago restaurants, where she was offered the prestigious position of head chef.

Christina and her family live in a spacious home in the Chicago area and she loves to grow her own vegetables and herbs in the garden she lovingly cultivates on her sprawling estate. Her and her husband have two beautiful children, 3 cats, 2 dogs and a parakeet they call Jasper. When Christina is not hard at work creating beautiful meals for Chicago's elite, she is hard at work writing engaging e-books of which she has sold over 1500.

Make sure to keep an eye out for her latest books that offer helpful tips, clear instructions and witty anecdotes that will bring a smile to your face as you read!

Made in the USA
Las Vegas, NV
14 December 2023